My View

Essays on Faith and Culture
From the Editorial Page of
The Cape Cod Times

Kent D. Moorehead

Portland • Oregon
INKWATERPRESS.COM

*Scan this QR Code
to learn more about
this title*

Publisher: Inkwater Press

Paperback
ISBN-13 978-1-59299-867-8 | ISBN-10 1-59299-867-4

Hardcover
ISBN-13 978-1-59299-869-2 | ISBN-10 1-59299-869-0

Kindle
ISBN-13 978-1-59299-868-5 | ISBN-10 1-59299-868-2

Printed in the U.S.A.
All paper is acid free and meets all ANSI standards for archival quality paper.

3 5 7 9 10 8 6 4 2

TO BISHOP C. DALE WHITE
a constant witness for peace and justice

Contents

Contents Continued

MY VIEW

INTRODUCTION

THE ESSAYS IN this small volume were all published by the *Cape Cod Times* in their My View column, which appears weekdays on the editorial page. The *Times* is the major newspaper on Cape Cod and the Islands of Martha's Vineyard and Nantucket, and it has a circulation of approximately fifty thousand. I am grateful to Mr. William Mills and his staff, who accepted these eleven essays covering a variety of topics. I have tried to be timely in my submissions corresponding to a season of the year, such as Christmas, and to current events, such as the Fort Hood shootings. The editors have been generous in publishing my essays even though the ideas and opinions expressed in them don't always agree with those of the paper. They have also kindly allowed me to use the paper's name in the title of this volume.

In drawing together these essays, I have added a reflection on all but the last essay. These reflections include my further thinking on the issue as well as comments, letters, and e-mails I have received in response to the original essays. Some of these essays were favorably received and the responses were positive; others caused something of a stir; and usually the responses were mixed. This was often more interesting to me.

The original My Views are reprinted here as they appeared in the paper. On the title page of each essay I have included the date of publication as well as the newspaper's summary pull-out.[1] The reflections have been expertly edited by Susan Bouse of Bouse Editorial. My wife Beth has been very helpful in many ways. Several people have suggested this project, but the original idea

---

1   Two of the My Views had no summary pull-outs. I have added my own to *Dining at the Royal Table* and *Respecting Animals on Earth Day.*

came from the late William Pendleton, who was a supporter and a tough critic. I miss Bill.

As you will see, these essays are "about" seasons or events, but the "topic" is always probed as a sort of gift that gives us the opportunity to grow through self-reflection and deeper thinking about the world around us and our place in it. Both the essays and the responses are driven by my own understanding of God, and I often use biblical stories to shed light on these topics. Thus, a word needs to written here about biblical interpretation. I take the Bible seriously but not literally. I am interested in the meaning of the stories and the texts. For instance, in the text that has Jesus walking on water, the question is not "how could this happen?" but "what is the meaning in this story?" Is there any support for us in the storms of life? In my early years, I tried to figure out how it could happen and struggled with whether I had to believe it literally to be in good graces with the church. Marcus Borg would also have us ask, "What kind of towering personality was Jesus that these stories were told about him?" So, whether it is the story of the three astrologers who visit with Herod or the Star of Bethlehem, I am always seeking the meaning of the text.

Thank you for considering My Views. The following is the My View format as it appears in the paper.

MY VIEW

Humanity influences rationality

By KENT MOOREHEAD

One of the most fascinating discussions following the nomination of Judge Sonia Sotomayor to the Supreme Court concerns the role of experience and feelings in making legal decisions. Implicit in this discussion is the ability of judges to make purely rational decisions when interpreting the Constitution.

On the one hand there are those who say this is possible and they often use phrases praising "strict constructionists" or warning us of "activist judges" One can almost get the image of disembodied brains behind the bench making purely computer-type rational decisions. On the other hand are those who say it is impossible to separate experience and feelings in decision making. Judge Sotomayor and Justice Samuel Alito have both indicated that they believe their life experiences help them make better judgments.

I believe it is impossible to

In our personal decisions we need to take into account our tendency to rationalize our self interests.

make purely rational decisions. It would be great if Hamlet was completely accurate when he stated in Shakespeare's famous play, "What a piece of work is man! How noble in reason. How infinite in faculty! ....in apprehension, how like a god!" Alas, while what he says is partly true, it is not the whole truth. For humans also have self interest and it motivates their decisions in life. People who believe it is possible to make decisions using their pure reason do it at the peril of self deception. If it were possible for the Supreme Court to make these pure decisions would not most decisions be 9-0? In fact, it is often possible to make fairly accurate predictions on how the justices will vote. There are other factors in play than pure intellect. I dare say that their values, political convictions, as well as other

factors are involved (for exciting bedtime reading on this subject try Immanuel Kant's Critique of Pure Reason).

I used to enjoy William F. Buckley's "Firing Line" on television. Buckley, intelligent and articulate, would often invite guests to debate important issues of the day. Many of these guests were also intelligent and articulate and round they would go for the duration of the show. It seemed reasonable to me that these highly intelligent people should be able to convince Buckley or vice versa. The reality was that very few minds were changed, and people left - the program with their positions in tact. It began to occur to me that something else was going on.

In reality, the mind is often at the service of the will. We often come out in our thinking where

we will ourselves to come out. This is true of common folk as well as Supreme Court justices. One of my professors used to describe this by using the illustration of the man who put his conscience in a wheelbarrow, and then as he pushed it where he wanted it to go asserted that he always followed his conscience.

This is not a counsel of despair. It is a corrective in decision making. It means that in our personal decisions we need to take into account our tendency to rationalize our self interests. When we do this, recognizing the influence of our experience and our values, we can factor that into the process and make better and less self-deceptive decisions. I believe the same is true of the Supreme Court. The test for the justices is whether they understand as they apprehend and reason that they are not gods but human.

The Rev. Dr. Kent Moorehead is a retired United Methodist minister. He lives in Brewster.

Chapter one

THAT AWFUL 'L' WORD

February 21, 2005

*Liberal is defined as a movement
in Protestantism that emphasized
Intellectual liberty and the spiritual
and ethical content of Christianity*

THAT AWFUL 'L' WORD

DURING THE RECENT presidential election I turned on one of the evening shows on Fox television in which there is usually a good deal of shouting. The young host was scowling and berating certain newspapers and certain politicians and certain kinds of churches that are dangerous to our nation. He kept using the same word over and over again and he used it as one might use a four-letter word.

It was the awful word "liberal". President Bush used it regularly in the recent campaign to tarnish his opponent, John Kerry. Apparently it worked, for he and others kept talking about liberals and people who were even "too liberal."

I decided to go to the dictionary to see what a liberal was so I would know one when I saw one and could protect myself and my church. Here is what this heinous and dastardly word means according to my American Heritage Dictionary: The first definition referred to the Latin root of the word, which was *libre*, which means free, and implies intellectual freedom. That didn't sound so terrible so I read on.

The next definition was "generous" or "giving freely." Not so bad, so I read more. The next was "broad-minded and tolerant of the views of others." So far so good.

The next definition really surprised me. Liberal means "favoring democratic or republican (small "d" and small "r") forms of government as opposed to monarchies or totalitarian states." We speak about the liberal democracies of Europe. Well, I was yet to find anything so horrible. I read on.

The next definition said liberal means "emphasizing the liberal arts, such as literature and music." Last, it defined liberal as a movement in Protestantism that emphasized intellectual liberty and the spiritual and ethical content of Christianity.

There is the story of the little boy who said, "When I first went to school I didn't know what a scholar was, and now I are one." Well, after reading the definition of liberal, I guess I are one, too. At least I wish I could live up to the definition. To put it negatively, I don't want to be closed-minded, stingy, intolerant of others, supportive of totalitarian forms of government, against the liberal arts, or opposed to the spiritual and ethical content of Christianity.

When we label people we often libel them and vilify them so I urge us to not take good words and misuse them. Look up conservative in the dictionary—is a good word also. When we label we also divert attention from the real issues of our world and, rather than talk about what counts we confuse. Wouldn't it be wonderful if we could have a moratorium on incrimination and have a serious dialogue in this country on the real issues that confront us?

REFLECTION

THIS WAS THE first essay of mine that was published by the *Cape Cod Times* and, along with "The Bones of Jesus" and "The Animated Life of Guns," it elicited the most vigorous reader response. Most of the responses were positive, but not all of them. The first letter I received clearly "put me in my place," the author claiming that my valiant effort to rehabilitate the word liberal would be "laughable were it not so pathetic." He also suggested that I demonstrated un-liberal-like bias in that he felt I implied that conservatives are narrow-minded and intolerant. The next letter I received came from a well-known conservative columnist who said that I might find it difficult to believe (which I did) that he agreed with me completely, but added "as one who uses liberal and liberalism pejoratively I reject 'limousine and plantation' liberalism in politics, the media and academia." He then ended his response saying, "thanks for the excellent essay."

I was actually heartened by these and other responses because they demonstrated that it is still possible to have a civil if somewhat terse discussion of the issues of liberalism and conservatism. For many others who commented on the essay, issues of labeling and misunderstanding were foremost. In my interview with Dean Walter Muelder of the Boston University School of Theology in the summer of 1997 issue of *Bostonia* magazine, he said that "liberalism is an epithet today, not an idea. Historically it meant to be in favor of free enterprise and it also supported those ideas that John Stuart Mill and others held in regard to civil liberties." He also went on to say that liberalism meant that one was open to challenges from science while retaining a basic loyalty to Christ.

My son Gary wrote that "there is a lot of worthy reflection and discussion to be had about the evolution of words; how we use words sometimes spin off into another meaning. Often the *denotation* gets lost in the *connotation*." *Awesome* is a good example of this: a word that was often reserved for grand or even celestial events is now used to describe hamburgers or movies. He also mentioned that there is an element of human nature that pushes us to intentionally misuse words to make our point. I have noticed that this is often the case in discussions of liberalism and conservatism. I must confess that my commitment to nonviolence is sorely tested when I hear political commentators or candidates intentionally misusing words to make their point. So, perhaps the first issue is to, as Dean Muelder often said, keep our categories clean. That is to "say what we mean." Several of the respondents to the essay remarked about the importance of clarity of definition. "Rational and clear voices need to be heard," was one response. The great preacher Dr. Henry Hitt Crane said this:

> The first principle of any intellectual progress that we can make is to insist upon definition of terms, before even we begin to discuss, for when we are reluctant to give precise meanings that may be accepted by both parties,

then we seem to be incapable of creating what we call a community of discourse.

A second issue is to practice what we preach or, as Dean Muelder would assert, "mean what we say." In the two early responses noted, liberals acting illiberally were mentioned negatively. If we proclaim freedom of expression for ourselves, we need to proclaim and support it for others, especially those with whom we disagree. Nevertheless, those who hold a liberal faith, while recognizing the legitimacy of differing views, need to proclaim their faith with confidence and enthusiasm and not be defensive because *liberal* in some circles is a word of ill repute. Paul Krugman, in his book *The Conscience of a Liberal*, says that many people now prefer to call themselves progressive rather than liberal because of the decades-long propaganda campaign that has been so successful in making Americans distain the word *liberal*. I continue to prefer *liberal* because it is a more expansive term than *progressive*, which is often narrowly identified with politics. Perhaps we can also redeem the word *evangelical* to include one of its early meanings of "proclaiming the Good News" and consider ourselves evangelical liberals proclaiming and practicing our faith.

Chapter two

DINING AT THE ROYAL TABLE

August 1, 2005

The task of the religious community is
to speak truth to power

DINING AT THE ROYAL TABLE

IT IS FASCINATING to see in our day ministers and other religious leaders being invited or courting invitations from the men and women of power to the so called "centers of power". It is equally intriguing to see these leaders, many of whom seem obsessed by issues of sexuality, being seduced with that ultimate aphrodisiac, power. Power is a great temptation for religious leaders and it is a heady experience. This is nothing new, for there have always been religious authorities seeking to influence the political realm from the inside. Often however, when they get on the inside or get invited to the Prayer Breakfast they, knowingly or not, end up serving the political powers and their agenda. Billy Graham, who was the most skilled religious leader of our time at being able to get on the inside to counsel and witness for his faith, may have not fully realized how he was being used by politicians.

The well-known biblical scholar Dr. Walter Brueggemann reminds us of a very instructive story in the Book of Daniel in the Hebrew Scriptures. Daniel and his friends are in exile in Babylon and they seem to be exceptionally attractive and healthy young people. They attract the attention of the king and receive an invitation to dine at the royal table and enjoy the royal rations. But Daniel knows the danger of this. Eat royal rations and you may well end up thinking royal thoughts. Eat royal bread and there is a tendency to embrace royal hopes. Dine at the royal table and you might just end up serving royal agendas. Identify with the oppressors and you might take on their identity without even realizing it. Although it must have been a very real temptation, Daniel refuses to capitulate. In our time, it often appears that religious leaders have become the mouthpiece of the political powers. Some want to be a mouthpiece for they believe their goals and the agenda of the current "powers that be" are the same. Others have been drawn in by their own ambition. Nevertheless each should take that old Chinese proverb into account, "He who rides the tiger dare not dismount".

The task of the religious community, to use the Society of Friends phrase, is to "speak truth to power". John F. Kennedy in his introduction to *Profiles in Courage* acknowledges that politics is the art of compromise. He says, "Even the necessity for the right kind of compromise does not eliminate the need for those idealists and reformers who keep our compromises moving ahead". When we play the insider game rather than speaking truth and challenging our leaders with grand visions, we often just end up whispering half-truths to less than half interested politicians.

Reflection

I'll never forget a lecture by Dr. Harrell F. Beck in my first year at The Boston University School of Theology. Beck was professor of Old Testament (as we called it in those days) and was a dynamic lecturer making Hebrew Scripture (as we call it today) come alive. The lecture was about the encounter of Ahab, Jezebel, and the prophet Elijah. Ahab was the king of Israel, and he admired a beautiful vineyard that was owned by a man named Naboth. Ahab desperately wanted the vineyard, but legally he couldn't have it. Jezebel, his wife, said "You're the king, find a way to take it." Ahab does figure a way, through treachery and dishonesty, to acquire the vineyard. Then, Dr. Beck dramatically told his vivid version of the story:

> Ahab comes into his newly acquired vineyard in the cool of the evening and settles in to relax and enjoy himself. Then he sees a figure in the mist and he knows it is Elijah, and he knows he is there to confront

him for his evil in God's sight. Ahab says to Elijah, "What are you doing here, you troubler of Israel?"

This is the beginning of the end of Ahab's kingdom.

I have, since that lecture in Boston so long ago, seen this story as one model of the way the religious community relates to the state. We are called to confront the "powers that be" when they participate in actions or policies that are evil. We are called to be "troublers of Israel." There are many examples of this, such as Moses confronting Pharaoh, Nathan challenging David, Jesus in the Temple troubling the money changers, the role of the church in the civil rights movement, and Senator Mark Hatfield "ruining" the Presidential Prayer Breakfast in 1973 by speaking out against the Vietnam War (Which earned him a place on President Nixon's enemies list). Carl Schurz, a nineteenth-century congressman, put it well when he said, "My country, right or wrong. When right to be kept right, when wrong to be put right." On occasion, it is "simply" a matter of telling the truth: Andrew Butterfield answering "yes" when asked whether there was a taping mechanism in the oval office and John Dean saying that there was a "cancer on the Presidency" transformed the Watergate investigation. Albert Camus once said that "a book is not true because it is revolutionary, it has a chance of being revolutionary only if it tries to tell the truth." We are called to "speak truth to power."

The Schurz quote also has a cautionary note for would-be prophets-troublers of Israel, especially those who just enjoy a good fight and like to make trouble. We are called to challenge the "powers that be" when things need to be put right, but also to support the powers when things they are doing need to be kept right. President Eisenhower integrating the Little Rock Public Schools and President Kennedy integrating the University of Alabama were loud calls for the support of the religious community. In fact, it is ironic that in 2012 the prophetic community needs to demonstrate vigorous support for the many good works (imperfect as they are) of the federal government such as Pell Grants and safety nets for the poor, as they now are coming under attack.

This calls to mind those who seek to work from inside or "dine at the royal table" in hopes of influencing those in power. This is a valid strategy, but in the previous essay I pointed out the dangers of being co-opted and used. The case of Billy Graham, who has managed to pray, advise, and consult with every president from Truman on, is quite complex because we don't know his motives or goals, or what went on behind the scenes. We do know from the release of the Nixon tapes that Graham supported Nixon's anti-Semitic rants not just with silence: In a taped conversation on February 1, 1972, Graham voiced openly his belief that Jews control the American media, saying, "This stranglehold has got to be broken or the country's going down the drain." Nixon responded positively, and then Graham said, "if you get elected a second time, then we might be able to do something." Martin Marty of the University of Chicago asked, "Did it ever occur to him [Graham] that he should have countered the President?" In an interview with *Christianity Today*, an evangelical monthly, Graham, in reflecting on his long life and public ministry, says, "I would have steered clear of politics. I am grateful for the opportunities that God gave me to minister to people in high places; people in power have spiritual and personal needs like everyone else... But looking back I know I sometimes crossed the line. I wouldn't do that now." Graham, like all of us, is vulnerable.

So, we walk a tightrope, wanting to be supportive of the state when we can and challenging the state when we must. Let us do it without arrogance and certainly avoiding simplistic answers to the complex and nuanced issues of our time.

Chapter three

GRACIOUS, GENEROUS TO THE END

April 24, 2006

William Sloane Coffin Jr. will be remembered for his preaching power, courage, musical talent and the immense role he played in the civil rights and peace movements

GRACIOUS AND GENEROUS TO THE END

ARTHUR MILLER ONCE said, "Bill Coffin is an American knight, a stranger to fear, the visionary's best companion, a joyfully embattled Christian, his life the richest imaginable." Rabbi Arnold Wolf called him "the single most gifted person I have ever met." Certainly, he will be remembered for his manifold gifts; his intellect, preaching power, courage, musical talent, and the immense role he played in the civil rights and peace movements. I will remember him for all of these things, but especially for his graciousness and generosity toward people.

I first experienced his graciousness during the student strikes, at Mt. Holyoke College, after the bombing of Hanoi in 1970. Bill came to speak at the chapel and participate in anti-war demonstrations. I was the minister of the United Methodist Church in South Hadley, and was taking part in the activities. Tamara Knell, director of the Glee Club, was apologizing to Bill for having to leave campus to direct a joint concert with the Yale Glee Club at Carnegie Hall. "I feel so guilty for not being here for the demonstrations", she said. Bill put his hands on her cheeks, looked at her, and said, "Tamara, you *must* go. Create beauty so we can always keep a vision of the kind of world we want, for we must love the good more than we hate the evil, or we will just end up being good haters."

Another experience was hearing The Rev. Dr. Carla Bailey, of Christ Church at Dartmouth, tell of Bill, a few months before the end of his life--his body failing but his mind sharp, giving an hour and a half of his precious time to talk with Dr. Bailey's high school age daughter about a paper she was writing on religion. He listened to her intently, asking questions about her ideas and her life. Then, with great sensitivity, he shared his convictions with her, never being condescending or judgmental. As he had done so beautifully while chaplain at Yale, he gave generously of his time.

I also remember a visit my wife Beth and I had with Bill at his home in Strafford, Vermont, a village just across the river from Dartmouth College, where Beth's daughter is the softball coach. We sat on the porch on a beautiful late summer day. He asked his son-in-law to get us a drink, and then asked us about our lives, wondering if I would "flunk retirement" and how Beth survived being a minister's spouse. He was especially interested in the Dartmouth softball team and the emergence of women's college athletics. Beth reports that she felt he truly was interested in her, an experience she doesn't always have in the presence of "important" people. It was a memorable afternoon.

Since that visit I would call Bill every other month or so and he, when I identified myself, would always ask, "How's the coach, how's the team?" I talked with him on the phone not long before he died. He was in hospice care and praised their work. He said, "I am ready to go. I have been around long enough and it's time to get out of the way and make room for others." A gracious and generous soul to the very end.

Reflection

Gary Trudeau, creator of the Doonesbury comic strip, spoke at an April 28th, 2005 dinner in honor of the public witness and ministry of William Sloane Coffin Jr. and told this story about a man who thought of himself as a moth: The man walked into a doctor's office and said he needed help. The doctor responded, "I am a general practitioner, and you need to see a psychiatrist." Whereupon the man replied, "Well, actually, I was on my way to see one, but I noticed your light was on." Trudeau recalled that this was the way it was with Coffin and hosts of students at Yale, including himself. We were on our way to something else and noticed his light, this astonishing incandescence of a warrior, pulling triple duty in the service of God, country, and Yale. One of those students on his way to the gym or somewhere else was Calvin Hill, who became a Yale football legend and star player for the Dallas Cowboys. He decided to stop at the beautiful Battell Chapel where he heard Coffin preach for the first time.

Hill became a Chapel deacon. "I didn't want be like [professional football hero] Jim Brown, said Hill. I wanted to be like Bill Coffin." So it is for many who have been drawn to his light.

Coffin was far from perfect, as his autobiography and several biographies show, but he possessed a dynamism and effervescence that was alluring. One of my lasting memories of him was in the pulpit at Riverside Church in New York, saying with great power that "God wants us to have joy!" He would say, "I love the recklessness of faith. First you leap and then you grow wings." Or he might ask, "Why are Christians so often joyless? It is, I think, because too often Christians have only enough religion to make them miserable." And then, of course, one of my favorite quotes of his that I used in the essay and in many sermons, "True we have to hate evil; else we're sentimental. But if we hate evil more than we love the good, we become damned good haters, and of those the world has too many." He made the faith attractive in the best sense of that word. He believed that religion was a wholehearted giving of oneself in love for God and for others.

His involvement in social causes was legendary and well documented. He considered himself an American patriot who loved his country enough to address her flaws and thought that preachers today worth their salt need to insist fearlessly that "God 'n' country" is not one word. He was concerned that in this world of pain, crying out for change, so many American churches today are basically doing little more than management and therapy.

In his later years, he became reflective and thought and wrote about the end of life: "I've noticed that the older, the more gnarled the cherry tree, the greater the profusions of blossoms. And sometimes the oldest and dustiest of bottles hold the most sparkling wine. I'm drawn by faces lined with crow's feet, those 'credentials of humanity,' beautifully lit from within."

It was during the last year of his life that Beth and I visited with him in Strafford, Vermont, where he and his wife, Randy, lived. It was a beautiful summer day, and we sat on the lovely porch that looked down to the village church. Bill was suffering from congestive heart failure and couldn't walk very well, but he was fully alert and engaged, and we talked for several hours. It was a bittersweet time, he, always the good listener, asked us questions about our lives and family. He talked about how important friendships[1] become in later years and how much closer he felt toward the environment now that he was about to join it. A typical Coffin comment! It was a day I will always remember.

He wrote in his book *Credo* that:

> Death is the great equalizer, not because it makes us equal, but because it mocks our pretensions at being anything else. In the face of death, differences of race, class, nationality, sexual orientation all become known for the trivial things they ultimately are. Finally, with no deaths there would long since have been no births, the world being overpopulated with immortal beings.

---

[1] Bill had many good friends, and I don't want to give the impression that I was one of them. I was an acquaintance.

Just think: Giotto maybe, but no Cezanne, let alone Andy Warhol; Purcell maybe, but no Bach, Beethoven, Brahms, let alone Aaron Copland; Roman gladiators yes, but no Sugar Ray Robinson or Muhammad Ali. And, of course, no you and me, no grandchildren!

Chapter four

The Bones of Jesus

March 15, 2007

*The controversy (over Jesus' tomb) has
the value of causing us to re-evaluate
our faith*

THE BONES OF JESUS

THE SENSATIONAL CONTENTION that the lost tomb of Jesus, which may contain his bones, has been discovered, is being called a threat to Christian faith. This alleged discovery is making provocative headlines and eliciting yet another controversy. The implication is, of course, that if Jesus didn't rise bodily from his tomb, as demonstrated by the discovery of his bones, then the whole of Christian faith is false. This is true only for those who base their faith on miracles such as the bodily Resurrection, walking on water, or the Virgin Birth. The truth is that millions of faithful Christians, lay and clergy, have believed for centuries that Jesus' resurrection was spiritual and not bodily. They do not base their faith on miracles. To lump all believers into the one camp of those who believe in the bodily Resurrection is a gross over simplification. To me the basis of Christian faith is not belief in miracles, but the faith, as St. Paul said, that God was in Jesus. The basis of faith is that there is a Divine Reality that has a character like the character of Jesus. One may also believe in fantastic and miraculous events but this is not fundamental to Christian belief.

It is unlikely, from my point of view, that much will come from this recent sensational "discovery", but the controversy has the value of causing us to re-evaluate our faith. Suppose it could be proven that the bones of Jesus have been discovered. What would that mean? It would mean that in Jesus we have a real flesh and blood human being who lived an extraordinary life. It would support the Bible's contention that Jesus was fully human. The fundamental faith question would still remain, do we believe that God was in Jesus giving us an amazing glimpse of what is most true about this universe. Rather than a defensive reaction to the claim that the lost tomb of Jesus has been found, let us see this latest "revelation" as a cause for growth---a stimulus to asking what is fundamental in the faith. We should always welcome a lively discussion of our basic convictions.

I believe that God is truth and the closer we get to truth the closer we are to God, or Ultimate Reality. If something is not true than the sooner we find out the better. Religious believers need to have no fear of the search for truth. To believe in unexamined dogmas and to refuse to change our minds in the face of new truths is in reality a danger to faith. It is not only spiritual rigamortis but is also one of the great stumbling blocks to healthy relationships with the adherents of other religions. It may also be one of the reasons for so much strife in our world. Mark Twain once said that "man is the only animal with the true religion---several of them." Perhaps it is time to give up our religious imperialistic and exclusivist positions and join with all humanity in the larger search for truth, thus bringing all of us closer to the Divine Reality.

REFLECTION

IT IS NOT surprising that there was a good deal of reaction to this essay. A retired Lutheran pastor said that I was only giving credence to present-day hoaxes. Actually, I never gave credence to the tomb of Jesus theory. I used it only as a way to think about Resurrection. He also wrote that, while there may be many who accept my viewpoint, still the bulk of Christian pastors on Easter preach a message of real Resurrection, and on Ascension Day, a real *bodily* ascension. A blogger posted a comment to this, asking, "Someone please tell me where a physical body could rise to." I chuckled when I first read this Internet communication, but in reality the question is an important one for those who take the biblical account literally. If you have a body, then what happens to it? If it ascends, where does it go? Where is Jesus now? Does he, as some apparently believe, have his own planet? Jesus as a living spiritual reality is another matter.

Another pastor of a Bible Church wrote his own My View in response to what I had written. This is highly unusual, as the *Cape Cod Times* seldom prints responses to My View articles. This letter said that my speculative assertions lack substance and credibility. He also went on to write that it is true that there are "millions" who do not believe in the physical Resurrection and that he would disagree that they should be labeled "Christians." He then said that he recognized what my real purpose was when I wrote about giving up our religious imperialistic and exclusivist positions and joining with all humanity in the search for truth. He believes that "Christian" truth is exclusive.

On the other hand, there were many positive responses. One had a very positive view of my imperialistic and exclusivist comments. A local rabbi wrote, saying, "I share your commitment to search for the larger truths which unite us all." The associate rector of a nearby Episcopal church asked if he could use it for his adult study (the article was published during Lent). He did and then called me afterward and said the class split

50-50 in agreeing and disagreeing with the article! There were a number of other responses, and it was encouraging to get both the pro or con calls and e-mails and to know that some people are still interested in religious dialogue.

This is my view: Jesus was alive in the early church as a *remembered person* and a *present power.* The church remembered him by sharing his teachings and stories of his life. Do you remember singing in Sunday school "Tell Me the Stories of Jesus"? The curriculum of the early church was telling and probably singing the stories and teachings of Jesus. There was no Bible or creeds at this time—only oral tradition, some written material, and some of the letters of Paul. The first of the four Gospels was not written until at least thirty years after Jesus's crucifixion, and the last, the Gospel of John, sixty to seventy years after the crucifixion. So the early church gathered to keep his memory alive. The church was also aware of a "presence" or a "spirit" that was alive in their midst. I believe the spirit they experienced was the spirit of God that was in Jesus. After his death, the church found that his spirit was alive and well. The Rev. Dr. William C. Trench says, in regard to the appearances, "Clearly we are not talking about a resuscitated corpse. The Gospel descriptions never confront the issue head on. When Paul describes his encounter on the road to Damascus he claims that the appearance to him is just the same as earlier appearances to other Disciples."

I believe the Resurrection was not a physical event, not a dead body being resuscitated, but the explosion of the Christ spirit that occurred at his death. A spiritual Resurrection means that we can experience Christ in the same way the early followers of Jesus did and not have a second-class Resurrection because we didn't experience the "real thing." For me, the words of Albert Schweitzer still resonate with the power of Resurrection:

> Jesus means something to our world because a mighty force streams forth from him and through our time also. It is the solid foundation of Christianity.

Chapter five

MOTHER THERESA, THE DOUBTER

August 30, 2007

We rarely doubt things that have little
or no importance to us

MOTHER TERESA, THE DOUBTER

TIME MAGAZINE HAS created a great deal of attention with its recent article on Mother Theresa. Apparently, she wrestled with doubts for many years and questioned the presence of God in her life. Many of us are like Mother Theresa, by which I mean we also have doubts. You may at this very moment be questioning the basis of your beliefs. You may be doubting that your life or your work is worthwhile.

In reality, doubt is not a lack of faith but a very important element of it. When a person in one of my churches would come to me expressing doubts, I knew they were beginning to take their faith seriously. We rarely doubt things that have little or no importance to us. Let us thank God for doubts. Sir Frances Bacon once said that "If we begin with certainties, we will end in doubt, but if we are content to begin with doubt we will end in certainty." Galileo went even further when he said that doubt "is the father of invention." Where would we be without the capacity to doubt? How could we grow?

Look at all the things that need to be doubted. Many of our heroes were people who were able to look at an injustice or an untruth and say, "I doubt it." Those who doubted that slavery was an inevitable institution were often the ones who led the fight for freedom. Many medical discoveries have come as the result of doubts. When Galileo doubted that the earth was the center of the universe, it led the way to a greater understanding of our place in the cosmos. Alfred Lord Tennyson said, "There lives more faith in honest doubt, believe me, than in half the creeds." There is no freedom of thought unless we have the freedom to doubt.

There is a kind of certainty that is harmful. Don't you wish some of our current "true believers" would have doubts serious enough to cause them to stop their deadly practices? Would that those who are killing for God these days could have some serious doubts. On the contrary, they seem "full of faith." I wish those who killed so many in the Oklahoma City bombing had doubted. Would that there had been serious doubting during the decision to attack Iraq. Apparently, many warnings of dire consequences were dismissed. Don't you wish that every young person, being told by a drug pusher that they will get high and happy, would have the capacity to doubt and then desist? This is the kind of doubt that can cause us to resist evil and error.

There is also the kind of doubt that comes from struggling with evil and wondering if it is all worth it, or if there is a God who cares. This seems to be the kind of doubting which Mother Theresa was experiencing. When things are going well it is easier to have faith. Sitting on a beach on Cape Cod on a perfect summer day lends itself to faith that life is good and God is good. Working with terrible poverty in the slums of Calcutta lends itself to doubts about the goodness of life and perhaps even the goodness of God. I would have been completely surprised if the Time Magazine article came to the conclusion that Mother Theresa never doubted. She was too sensitive for that.

One more thing for all of us doubters. Harry Emerson Fosdick spoke wisely about the importance of being consistent in our doubting. He said if we doubt ourselves, our faith, and that the world can change its' violent ways, then it is also important to have the intellectual honesty to be fair and doubt our doubts as well. This is often the beginning of greater faith.

Reflection

Many years ago on a radio talk show, a woman asked a hostile question of The Reverend Jack Mendlesohn, pastor of the Arlington Street Unitarian Church in Boston. She said, "I know who you are [a Unitarian] and I want you to give me a simple yes or no answer to my question. Do you believe in God?" There was a pause, and Mendlesohn responded, "Describe God for me, and I will tell you whether I believe in the God you describe." A lively discussion followed. I found a version of this exchange to be helpful in my churches. When a young person was struggling with their faith and not sure he or she believed in God, it was helpful to ask, "Tell me what kind of God you don't believe in?" After he or she described a God who was an old man in the sky who watches over us, or the heavenly policeman who judges us, I would say, "I don't believe in that kind of God either. Let's talk about this."

Questions are so important. When I came as a first-year seminarian to Boston University, President Harold Case had a tradition of inviting new students to his home for a time of fellowship and sharing. It is one of my cherished memories of my time in Boston. We gathered on and around a great spiral staircase that graced the foyer of the "Castle" as the president's home was called, and Dr. Case said, "I have a question to ask of you." My immediate and silent response was that I didn't come all the way to Boston for questions...I came for answers! He asked it anyway. The question was: if you had to spend the rest of your life on a distant planet and could only take three books, which three would you take?

That question made us think about our values, goals, and dreams. That one excellent question was worth a thousand answers.

The purpose of a really good school is not to help students who come in with questions to leave with all the right answers but, rather, to help students ask the right questions. This is especially true in a seminary, where many of the students think they have the answers already. Learning answers takes memory; learning the right questions takes wisdom. Think of how often Jesus answered a question with another question.

Do you want to be healed?
Who do you say that I am?
Which of these was the neighbor?

Good questioning opens us up to creative thinking and to growth. Having all the answers ends growth. I agree with Bill Coffin, who said, "Believing that all things worth knowing are already known...preachers create an atmosphere of cultivated ignorance."

In this regard, it is especially important in thinking about Mother Teresa's struggles to ask the right questions. When you hear her anguish, it is not that of someone who is just having intellectual doubt, a kind of cerebral questioning. Read her own words in the book *Mother Teresa: Come be My Light*: "There is no One to answer...no one on Whom I can Cling...no, No One...alone...where is my faith...even deep down right in here there is nothing, but emptiness...and darkness...My God...how painful is this unknown pain...I have no faith."

These words are akin to what the existential-ists call "The Dark Night of the Soul." The right question to ask is beyond intellectual uncertainty. It is about what was bedeviling her.

In the essay, I suggested that there is a kind of doubt that comes from struggling with evil and wondering about the reality of a God of goodness, a God who cares about suffering, a God of justice. In her writings, she tends to identify her struggle with faith, not when she was in seminary or in her early years, but during her time in Calcutta. Under the terrible circumstances in which she ministered, who wouldn't find having faith in a just God difficult? As I suggested in the essay, it is one thing when things are going well, when the weather is perfect and the beach is so alluring, to have a kind of benign faith that all is good and even perhaps that God is mostly concerned about my career and my prosperity. It is another when you minister in the vast and seemingly hopeless slums of Calcutta.

Martin Luther King Jr. often quoted a phrase that originated from the great Boston preacher Theodore Parker:

The moral arc of the universe is long but
it bends toward Justice.

I suggest that to believe this was a major part of her struggle. It certainly is an important part of my faith struggle. Christian faith is more about acting and doing than just intellectual assent to a set of beliefs or doctrines. To her credit, even with her doubts, Mother Teresa continued her work and did her part to make the moral arc of the universe more just. We can all do the same. As Ann Frank wrote:

How wonderful it is that nobody need wait
a single moment before starting to improve
the world.

Chapter six

What Made the Wise Men Wise

December 17, 2007

They sensed the danger of Herod's newfound religiosity. They realized he was going to use them

WHAT MADE
THE WISE MEN WISE

WE OFTEN HEAR, during the Christmas season, that materialism undermines the true meaning of the season. There is some truth in this, but materialism, as a philosophy of life, falsifies the human struggle in any season, not just at Christmastime. In my view, what really undermines the deeper meanings of this season is the *sentimentalizing of the central stories of Christmas*. Certainly, many of the Christmas stories contain images of hope, love, and peace, and they are especially helpful for children. But these stories often have deeper meanings which speak to a maturing faith. A good example is the story of the Magi visiting the Holy Family. This familiar story is often sentimentalized into a kindly visit by three foreigners bringing gifts to a lovely family, surrounded by friendly animals, in a cozy stable. It is the stuff of which Hallmark cards are made.

In reality, the visit of the Magi is one surrounded by political intrigue and danger. According to the story, they had visited with Herod who, being threatened by this new birth, wanted to kill the child. He asks the Magi to come back and tell him where the child is so he can come and "worship" him. Apparently they considered this and then (warned in a dream of Herod's treachery) went home by another way. What made the wise men wise is that they sensed the danger of Herod's new found religiosity. They realized that he was going to use them and they decided not to fall prey to him.

I believe there is a lesson for our time in this story. We live in a political climate with the specter of many of our candidates, politicians and government leaders, wearing their religion on their sleeves, vying for the "religious vote." Beware when Herod, or the politicians, get religion. Politicians are not called to be publicly *pious* but to be *just.* When government leaders get religion, it is a religion that usually ends up serving the leaders' agendas. Political leaders over the centuries have been adept at appropriating the chief symbols of a faith and then acting diametrically opposite to the central values of the same faith. We will see this in this Christmas season as governmental authorities call on us to praise the Prince of Peace and also to keep on passing the ammunition of war. State religion is almost always ceremonial rather than ethical. Religion which knowingly or blindly serves the purposes of the government will eventually become the religion of the government in a de facto alliance with Caesar.

When our brilliant Founding Fathers wrote into our Bill of Rights the clause of the separation of Church and State they were not trying to save the State from the Church, but were seeking to protect the Church from the undue control of the State. They had seen enough of State religion in the Old World and wanted none of it. Czars and Kings were the head of not only the State but the Church as well, and it rendered religion the impotent servant of Czar and King. To the credit of the framers of our Constitution, they sought in the First Amendment to save us from State domination of religion.

So remember what made the wise men wise; they sensed the danger of Herod's new found "faith" and resisted him. When we sentimentalize an important story like the journey of the Magi, seeing it only as a nostalgic tale of thee kindly gentlemen making a benign visit to the manger on Christmas Eve, we miss one of the deeper meanings of the season.

Reflection

This essay is obviously a companion piece to "Dining at the Royal Table." It drew a good deal of positive feedback as well as one cautionary response. One minister asked for permission to use it in his monthly newsletter. My favorite was from a minister who said that the essay was worth the price of the paper. The *Cape Cod Times* at that time sold for fifty cents! Nevertheless, I took it as a compliment. The cautionary note came from a respected ministerial colleague, the Reverend Bob Moore. He wrote, "On the separation of church and state, I think it goes both ways. The public needs to be protected from the establishment of a state church." I did emphasize the church being protected from government control but as Rev. Moore implies, there is a need to be alert, as there is a growing movement calling for a form of theocracy. *Theos* is the Greek word for God and *cratein* means to rule. In a theocracy, the state is to be ruled by or be subject to religious authority.

There is a movement among Protestant Christian evangelicals and fundamentalists to not only encourage active participation by their adherents in civic society but also to seek to dominate the political process as part of a mandate from God. In 2005 at a "Reclaiming America for Christ" conference, the late D. James Kennedy, pastor of Coral Ridge Ministries, called on his followers to exercise "godly dominion...over every aspect...of human society":

> Our job is to reclaim America for Christ, whatever the cost. As the vice regents of God, we are to exercise godly dominion and influence over our neighborhoods, our government, our literature and arts, our sports arenas, entertainment media, our news media, our scientific endeavors—in short, over every aspect and institution of human society.

It is difficult to discern the strength of this movement. Bill Moyers, well-known journalist and television host, believes that people of faith have always tried to bring their convictions to bear on American laws and morals and that this is the American way encouraged and protected by the First Amendment. Moyers then goes on to say:

> But what is unique today is the radical religious right has succeeded in taking over one of America's great political parties. The country is not yet a theocracy but the Republican Party is and they are driving American politics, using God as a battering ram.

Others would say that it is not about traditional Republicans or conservative Christians but the far-right wing of the party. We did see in the recent presidential primary several candidates make statements that sounded perilously close to calling for religious control or dominion over the state. Theocracy folks not only believe that they have access to the mind of God but that God shares their political views. This issue bears close scrutiny, and wise folk need to be wary.

In this regard, we need to be wary of allowing any nostalgia we may have for this story to overwhelm us. This story of the Magi visiting Jesus and his parents and then discerning the danger from Herod, as I said in the essay, is always in danger of being sentimentalized. When we do this, we are in danger of losing the deeper meanings of this and other biblical stories. Frederick Buechner in his book *Telling the Truth* says it well:

> To sentimentalize something is to look only at the emotion in it and at the emotion it stirs in us rather than the reality of it...to sigh over the prettiness of it rather than to tremble at the beauty of it, which may make fearsome demands of us...Christians in general are particularly given to sentimentalizing our faith as much of Christian art and preaching bear witness—The sermon as tearjerker, the Gospel an urn of long stemmed- roses and baby's breath to brighten up the front of the church and Jesus as Gregory Peck.

What I try to do with this wonderful story is to accept the emotion it stirs in me with memories of childhood and merry Christmases with my family but also be aware that there are deeper meanings to be discerned that speak to my adult faith.

Chapter seven

CHRISTMAS MIRACLE ISN'T THE STAR

December 22, 2008

The heavenly conjunction may have actually been there, but it didn't validate Jesus. He did not need a star to affirm him

Christmas Miracle Isn't the Star

I HAVE ALWAYS been charmed by the story of the Star of Bethlehem and the visit of the Magi, astrologers who followed the star to the manger. I can recall as a child being fascinated both by the star which crowned our Christmas tree, our crèche with the Magi gazing reverently and that great star in the heavens (in our case it was a small light bulb above the crèche). It seemed to validate the importance of Jesus. Not only was it an important part of my childhood faith but a favorite symbol of the Christian faith. I will still be captured by the beauty and power of that star of wonder and light and hope again this Christmas Eve.

As I grew I honored my childhood faith but wanted to make it mature and thoughtful. I recalled how the Bible said that Jesus grew in wisdom. If he had something to learn, I certainly did too. I was also convinced that I could love God with my mind, so it was important to revisit the star as an adult. I found it difficult to believe that a Divine Being, knowing that Jesus was to be born, moved planets around to create a great "star." I also shared Albert Schweitzer's questioning, as a youth, the fact that the Magi never returned to inquire of Jesus and what Jesus' family, who were said to be poor, did with the gold and the other valuable presents they were given. I also learned that the story of the star appears only in the Gospel of Matthew which was written 80 years after the birth of Jesus.

It began to look as if my nativity scene was going to be a few camels shy. I began to feel a bit the way I felt when I realized that George Washington didn't throw a silver dollar across the Potomac. There were no silver dollars in his time and besides the river was a mile wide. Then a wise man reminded me that even if he didn't make that mighty toss he was still the great George Washington, the father of our country. His greatness in a way validated the familiar story. I am in no way equating Washington with Jesus but the wise man's *line of thought* intrigued me. So I did some more research.

I learned that in ancient times special importance was given to events in the "heavens." People read the "horoscope" (Greek *hora* meaning "hour" and *skopos* meaning "watcher"). When there was a particularly spectacular celestial display it was thought that a great leader or a messianic person had been born. When a great person emerged in history the astrologers looked backward to affirm that this person's destiny was in the stars. I also learned that Saturn and Jupiter were in conjunction in the sign of Pisces, the Fish, three times in 7 B.C. and that the year 6 B.C. brought a more unusual vision, for the planet Mars joined Saturn and Jupiter. These are also the approximate dates that modern scholars give to the birth of Jesus. So around the time of Jesus' birth there *was* a great heavenly light show.

My view is that as people began to recognize the importance of Jesus and some being aware of the celestial events around the time of his birth, connected these two events. The heavenly conjunction may have actually been there but it didn't validate Jesus. He did not need a star to affirm him. His life and incredible influence makes his birth and the celestial events, whether they coincided or not, an important part of our Christmas tradition. After all, the miracle of Christmas is not the appearing of angels or a mysterious star. The miracle is that the birth of a child, born in a barn to impoverished parents, in an out of the way backwater town, has brought such hope to humanity. As Schweitzer said, "a mighty force streams forth from him and flows through our time also." It is the character and influence of Jesus that validates the Star of Bethlehem.

REFLECTION

I WANT TO follow up on the concluding comments in this essay:

> The miracle is that the birth of a child, born in a barn to impoverished parents, in an out-of-the-way backwater town, has brought such hope to humanity. It is the character and influence of Jesus that validates the star of Bethlehem.

The December 6, 1999, issue of *Time* magazine had on its cover a painting by Antonelio da Messina, a fifteenth-century artist. It was titled *Christ at the Pillory.* Next to the face of Jesus was the title of the lead article, "Jesus at 2000." The article began with these words:

> The memory of any stretch of years eventually resolves to a list of names, and one of the useful ways of recalling the past two millenniums is by listing the people who acquired great power. Mohammed, Catherine the Great, Marx, Gandhi, Hitler,

Roosevelt, Stalin, and Mao come quickly to mind. There is no question that each of those figures changed the lives of millions and invoked responses from worship through hatred. It would require much exotic calculation, however, to deny that the single most powerful figure—not merely in these two millenniums but in all of human history—has been Jesus of Nazareth. Jesus Christ has cast a long shadow on history.

And, of course, he still does. Illustrations abound in our time of the enormous influence of Jesus. A relatively recent one comes from what many assume is a citadel of cynicism: Harvard. The last course at Harvard on the life of Jesus was taught by the great George Santayana in 1912. In 1982, the school decided to try again. Harvey Cox (an outstanding teacher and scholar) offered a course titled Jesus and the Moral Life. To the astonishment of the administration, the course drew great numbers of students. Early enrollment was so high the course had to be moved from a basement seminar room to a larger lecture hall to accommodate the four to eight hundred students who applied each semester. Finally, when the enrollment reached one thousand, the course had to be moved to Sanders Theater! What was fascinating was that the students who enrolled were Christian, Hindus, Buddhists, Muslims, and Jews, as well as agnostics and atheists.

Jesus's influence is still an eternal mystery. It is stunning and remarkable. This is not to say that we are number one, that we win. We who seek to follow this Jesus need not be arrogant. Many who are interested in Jesus are not interested in our version of his church and never will be. The church has a long way to go to catch up with Jesus and we don't need any more Christian triumphalism.

Allow me two personal comments. First, like many children raised in the church and in a Christian home, I learned that Jesus loved me. In fact I *knew* he loved me. As I look back on this now I realize, because of this, I, early in my life, had a profound sense of belonging here on earth. This has been an important anchor for me in times that were good and not so good. In case this sounds a little corny and naïve, remember that when the great theologian Karl Barth was asked to summarize his ominous *Church Dogmatics*, he responded, saying, "Jesus loves me this I know, for the Bible tells me so." I have often thought, over the years, of how Jesus could still love me. Is he "up" in heaven somewhere with sandals and a beard, loving me? Is he still the young Jesus of my childhood? What I have come to believe is that there has been a Creative Spirit of love surging through Creation, and for a time, Jesus embodied or incarnated that Spirit. He is gone in earthly form, but the Spirit is still here and active.

A second personal comment is that over the years as I have struggled to grow, I have come in touch with another aspect of the spirit of Jesus. He is loving and gentle but is also something else. He is a refiner's fire (to use the words of Malachi 3.2, immortalized in Handel's *Messiah*). He challenges us to grow up. He confronts our sick society, our petty prejudices, our materialisms and exclusivist tendencies. He confronts us in the poor and in those who, in our eyes, are a little "queer." I like things the way they are. I love a sunset over Cape Cod Bay, and I prefer not to be bothered or disturbed. It would be much more comfortable if Jesus stayed back in history or in some remote heaven. But the Spirit is still active in our midst.

The star of Bethlehem still shines.

Chapter eight

HUMANITY
INFLUENCES
RATIONALITY

July 2, 2009

*In our personal decisions we need
to take into account our tendency to
rationalize our self-interest*

HUMANITY INFLUENCES RATIONALITY

ONE OF THE most fascinating discussions following the nomination of Judge Sonia Sotomayor to the Supreme Court concerns the role of experience and feelings in making legal decisions. Implicit in this discussion is the ability of judges to make purely rational decisions when interpreting the Constitution.

On the one hand there are those who say this is possible and they often use phrases praising "strict constructionists" or warning us of "activist judges" to illustrate their views. One can almost get the image of disembodied brains behind the bench making purely computer type rational decisions. On the other hand are those who say it is impossible to separate experience and feelings in decision making. Judge Sotomayor and Justice Samuel Alito have both indicated that they believe their life experiences help them make better judgments.

In my view, I believe it is impossible to make purely rational decisions. It would be great if Hamlet was completely accurate when he stated in Shakespeare's famous play, "What a piece of work is man! How noble in reason. How infinite in faculty!... in apprehension, how like a god!" Alas, while what he says is partly true, it is not the whole truth. For humans also have self-interest and it motivates their decisions in life. The person who believes it is possible to make decisions using their pure reason does it at the peril of self-deception. If it were possible for the Supreme Court to make these pure decisions would not most decisions be 9-0? In fact, it is often possible to make fairly accurate predictions on how the justices will vote. There are other factors in play than pure intellect. I dare say that their values, political convictions, as well as other factors are involved (for exciting bedtime reading on this subject try Immanuel Kant's *Critique of Pure Reason*).

I used to enjoy William F. Buckley's *Firing Line* on television. Buckley, intelligent and articulate, would often invite guests to debate important issues of the day. Many of these guests were also intelligent and articulate and round they would go for the duration of the show. It seemed reasonable to me that these highly intelligent people should be able to convince Buckley or vice versa. The reality was that very few minds were changed and people left the program with their positions intact. It began to occur to me that something else was going on.

In reality, *the mind is often at the service of the will.* We often come out in our thinking where we will ourselves to come out. This is true of common folk as well as Supreme Court Justices. One of my professors used to describe this by using the illustration of the man who put his conscience in a wheelbarrow and then as he pushed it where he wanted it to go asserted that he always followed his conscience.

This is not a counsel of despair. It is a corrective in decision making. It means that in our personal decisions we need to take into account our tendency to rationalize our self-interests. When we do this, recognizing the influence of our experience and our values, we can factor that into the process and make better and less self-deceptive decisions. I believe the same is true of the Supreme Court. The test for the justices is whether they understand as they apprehend and reason that they are not gods but human.

Reflection

Two assertions were made in the previous essay: one, that we need to take into account our *tendency* to rationalize our self-interest and the other, that as we apprehend and reason, we need to understand that *we are not gods*. Reinhold Niebuhr, the great theologian (although he called himself an ethicist rather than a theologian) is very helpful in this matter. One of his most famous quotes is:

> Man's capacity for justice makes democracy possible, but his inclination to injustice makes democracy necessary.

Niebuhr's use of the word *inclination* is a reference to our human nature. We have a capacity for the good but also an inclination for evil or injustice, or perhaps we can even be so bold to use that confusing little word *sin*. The great gift of Niebuhr's writing is that he rescues the concept of sin from what he would call its "primitive distortions." These distortions involve sin as naughtiness or individual misbehavior. In this regard, I suspect that, most people when they hear the word *sin* think of sex. Our culture, through a relentless assault in the media, especially advertising, undergirds this notion. If I said that a very sinful woman or man lives in my neighborhood, people would probably think of some sexual issue rather of that person being a racist or treating others unjustly.

Niebuhr wrote about sin as arrogance, selfishness, pride, or assuming too much about oneself (confusing ourselves with God). On the individual level, he said that there is no more dangerous person than the one who believes he or she can read God's mind, is executing God's will, and has divine sanction for his or her opinions and actions. For Niebuhr, there is *relativity* in all human perspectives. On the national level, he wrote about our myth of national innocence, which he called delusional messianism. In fact, our human inclination for evil is much more dangerous on a corporate or national level.

As I write this, the Supreme Court has just announced its decision to uphold the Affordable Care Act. The idea that nine justices just using their intellects made this decision is clearly a wish dream. Justice Thomas and his wife received a large amount of money for her (and his) opposition to the Affordable Care Act. He had been asked to recuse himself but refused, apparently contending he could be objective. Justice Kagan had also worked in support of health care before she became a justice but didn't recuse herself either. After the decision, Justice Scalia, who was in the minority, made an angry statement that revealed his emotional involvement. The editors at *Time* magazine were so sure that they knew how eight of the justices would vote that their June 18, 2012, edition had a photo of Justice Anthony Kennedy on the cover, calling him the decider. They were almost right. Chief Justice Roberts surprised almost everyone by siding with the "liberals" on the court. The July 16, 2012, edition of *Time* magazine had a special report that involved a lengthy discussion of the many factors that went into Justice Robert's decision. I am not writing this to criticize the court's decision making, but I do believe it is a good example of Niebuhr's concept of relativity in all human perspectives and a good corrective to any sense of innocence we may have about the high court.

In this regard, the church, if it could get over its obsession with its "primitive distortions" of sin, including its hang-ups over sexuality, has an important message to proclaim. A religious analysis cuts deeper than any secular analysis of our culture. We recognize that we are not God and that we have an inclination or tendency to do evil as well as to do the good. Most churches in their liturgy openly admit their human imperfections. We, usually in the early part of the service, have a time of confession, a time when we cease from pretending and take off our masks. It's almost like saying "Let's deal with this up front so in the rest of the service we can call on our better nature without being naïve about ourselves." When we presume to speak to the world, we can do so acknowledging the "inclinations" of humanity, challenging any sense of innocence, and especially speaking "truth to power" when individuals or nations believe they have divine sanction to execute God's will.

Chapter nine

THE ANIMATED LIFE OF GUNS

December 2, 2009

Guns are inanimate objects, but humans animate or give life to them. Guns in the hands of a potential mass murderer, become enablers and partners

THE ANIMATED LIFE OF GUNS

THE SHOOTINGS AT Fort Hood are not the first and, sadly, probably will not be the last mass murders in our country. There seems to be an epidemic of violence in our nation and there seems to be no end to it. Mayor Richard Daley of Chicago named our "love affair with guns" as a causal factor of the terrible tragedy at Fort Hood. He joins those who see the availability of guns in great numbers and their availability to disturbed people as an important source of the problem. Immediately pro gun advocates responded with their slogan, which is almost an article of faith, "guns don't kill people, people kill people." In this view if a person wants to kill someone and they don't have a gun they will use a knife, club, or any available means.

In my view, each of these positions is an over-simplification. The truth lies somewhere in the middle. The reality is that *people kill people with the aid of guns.* In the midst of a mass murder the shooter and the gun are inseparable.

Guns are inanimate objects but humans animate or give life to them. Guns, in the hands of a potential mass murderer, become *enablers* and *partners.* The alleged shooter at Fort Hood had two FN Herstal five-seven pistols, often referred to as cop killers because of their lethal properties. Very likely these weapons emboldened the alleged shooter and led him to believe that he could carry out his "mission." It is hard to imagine that the killings at Fort Hood could have been carried out with knives or clubs. In like manner the mass murders at Columbine High School, Virginia Tech, Binghamton, and even the assassination of President Kennedy could not have been carried out without the partnership and enabling properties of the guns that were used.

Some of these killers may have been not just disturbed but also cowardly people in the sense that they would never consider engaging someone in hand to hand combat but who were willing to use guns at a distance.

For many responsible people guns are instruments that might protect them or enable them to go on hunting trips or go target shooting with friends and family. For disturbed people, the gun can become a tool of revenge or a way to make a personal or political statement.

In this respect we don't need to apologize in calling for reasonable gun control such as waiting periods, background checks, and limiting the availability of assault weapons that troubled or desperate people use in mass murders. Because potential mass murderers often give warning signals, raising awareness when people speak or act irrationally can also be a way of decreasing the number of incidents of violence. For instance in the case of Fort Hood the alleged shooter had made threatening or questionable statements and had recently purchased a second pistol. It should have been enough cause for concern and an inquiry by the proper legal authorities, that also protected his Constitutional rights, might have averted the tragedy.

Certainly, the shooter in the Fort Hood murders bears full responsibility for his actions, but the weapons he used, because of their lethal nature, were partners, enablers and I would suggest even encouragers in his "mission." They gave him the hope that he could be "successful." He couldn't have done it without them.

Reflection

As you might suspect, there were a number of fascinating responses to this essay. First, a number of the responses illustrated how a title (or a headline) can prejudice a reader almost to the point where it's as if he or she were wearing blinders. The *Cape Cod Times* reserves the right to change the titles of My Views essays, and they have indeed changed the titles of at least half the essays appearing here. They usually change them for the better. The title they gave this one was "Without Guns, No Mass Murders," and it proved to be misleading. I did not say that mass murders would be impossible without guns. The paper's summary pull-out quotation is what I intended to say:

> Guns are inanimate objects, but humans animate or give life to them. Guns, in the hands of a potential mass murderer, become enablers and partners.

In fact, in the fifth paragraph, I deliberately mentioned responsible people who might use a gun to protect themselves or to hunt or for target shooting. Apparently, a number of responders didn't read as far as this paragraph—or the title blurred their vision. Many fervently declared their right to protect themselves and their families. One wrote that I had made a compelling case with which he strongly disagreed. "I reserve the right to defend my family, myself and my property," he added. One blogger even created a line drawing of my house and said if he lived next door and an attacker came, he, while defending his house with his gun, would not defend mine.

Which leads me to a second comment. As many of you know, bloggers often use strong language and personally attack others. It seems that given the impersonal nature of the computer, it is easier to do this. My experience was no exception. Here are a few examples:

> "Pastor Moorehead is another of what passes for a religious 'leader' these days, and is nothing more than a Judas goat who'll lead his flock into the slaughter-house."

> "Utter crap!"

"Moorehead doubtless considers the unarmed millions who were butchered by Stalin, Hitler, Mao, Pol Pot...to be some kind of 'holy martyrs' that were sacrificed at the altar of pseudo-pacifism."

These bloggers obviously hadn't read or understood the fifth paragraph of the essay.

What is clear is that the subject of guns and gun control causes emotions to run high. We are dealing with issues of control, power, and masculinity. Which is to say is that responsible gun-control laws are going to be hard to put in place largely because the whole issue is surrounded by emotion and lack of clear thinking. Politicians run away from the issue and in the recent campaigns have felt the need to have photo ops of them hunting and bearing arms. Even the campaign of John Kerry, a decorated Vietnam veteran, wanted to show the candidate this way. There are a number of people who sincerely believe that the government will be coming for their guns. One blogger wrote that when they come for him they will have to (apparently quoting Charlton Heston) "pry his gun from his cold dead hands." Heston passed away a few years ago, and no one had come to pry his guns from his hands. At his death, his guns were firmly under his control. Nevertheless, there is a fear abroad that if President Obama, who mentioned in his campaign that he supports bans on assault weapons, is reelected, he will press for stricter controls, and if guns cannot be limited, ammunition might be.

As I write this, another mass murder has taken place in a motion picture theater in Aurora, Colorado, and a panel on a major television station is discussing why it is so hard to talk at all about gun control. Politicians seem to be cowering in fear of the gun lobby. Both candidates for president have appropriately spoken consoling words to the victims and their families, but Michael Bloomberg, mayor of New York City, has said that "soothing words are not enough. We want to know what they are going to do." Bloomberg believes that guns need to be kept out of the hands of criminals, the mentally ill and children. He also believes that there is no reason for civilians to have assault weapons whose only purpose is to kill people. I support his views. I also support the recent calls for limits on assault weapons, and the governor of Illinois who said he will seek legislation on this matter. It is important to make a distinction between classes and purposes of guns. For instance, I believe that the framers of the Second Amendment to the Constitution envisioned guns for use for self-defense, hunting and for being part of a well-regulated militia but they couldn't have imagined that all citizens could or should have assault weapons.

In the past, presidents and politicians have led in the matter of gun control. In 1989, following a mass shooting in Stockton, California, George H. W. Bush issued an executive order halting the importation of semi-automatic firearms. He based his order on the 1968 Gun Control Act. In 1994 Bill Clinton signed into law a ten year ban on assualt weapons. Ronald Reagan supported both of these acts. The ban died in 2004. In doing research, I also came across this article from the *Seattle Times*:

Former President George Bush (H. W.) a gun enthusiast and decades-long member of the National Rifle Association, has resigned from the group because of its statements that agents of the Bureau of Alcohol, Tobacco and Firearms are "jackbooted thugs" who harass gun owners.

Bush said that the attack on federal agents deeply offended his sense of decency and honor and his concept of service to country.

Dare we hope that more leaders might surface again to deal with responsible gun control? Perhaps even more politicians might be willing to risk support and take a stand. We need to support them when they do. And dare we hope that, in light of the seemingly endless episodes of gun violence, the people might rise up to support saner policies.

Chapter ten

RESPECTING ANIMALS ON EARTH DAY

April 23, 2010

A sentient being is a being with an interest in continuing to live, has feelings, can suffer, and can experience happiness and sadness

Respecting Animals on Earth Day

SEVERAL YEARS AGO I participated in a wonderful *Blessing of the Animals* service. It was a lovely early spring day, and as we gathered in a church court-yard adults, youth and children, brought their special animals to be blessed. There were dogs and cats, of course, but also rabbits, gerbils, birds, and turtles and others I have forgotten. I was amazed at how well they all got along with each other. It was almost as if they had some sense of the significance of the occasion. I was reminded of the Society of Friends vision of the Peaceable Kingdom. It was moving to see a visible expres-sion of the concept that animals are also creatures of God. It was also moving to see people with such caring attitudes toward animals.

When I arrived home in the early afternoon the thought occurred to me that many of the folks at that service of blessing would sit down with their families say a another blessing and then proceed to eat an animal or two. And not just some ferocious wild beast, but lambs, birds, pigs, cows and perhaps even a rabbit. Animals are not just things, they are sentient beings. A sentient being is a being with an interest in continuing to live, has feelings, can suffer, and can experience happiness and sadness. Pigs, for instance, are apparently quite intelligent and aware. Those of us who have had beloved pets recognize that animals are sentient beings.

We have in recent years also become aware of the suffering animals are subjected to in laboratories and factory farms. The animals that arrive at our dining tables have often led lives of pain and suffering. And we have also seen in our time awful examples of animal cruelty both in our country and around the world. I wonder if there is a connection between how we treat and have treated animals and the culture of violence in our world that extends to humans. Leo Tolstoy once said "As long as there are slaughterhouses there will be battlefields." I don't believe he meant that if people became vegetarians there would be no wars. Pol Pot was probably a vegetarian. I believe he meant that a culture of cruelty certainly contributes to increased cruelty making it easier to dehumanize our enemies.

So my modest proposal is that on April 22nd, the fortieth anniversary of Earth Day, we call a moratorium on eating any of God's creatures and decrease their suffering for at least one day. We might find that in doing so we may feel some solidarity with our animal brothers and sisters and continue the practice. I am aware that this simple proposal might be unpopular. I have been in conversations in which people were civil in discussing issues of war and peace, economics, and even religion but when issues of eating animals came up emotions were high, as if our masculinity or humanity or dominance over the beasts of the earth was being challenged. Nevertheless, let us take a day off and thereby give our fellow animal sentient beings a day off on Earth Day.

Reflection

That this piece was published at all surprised me, as I believed it would never be accepted. Actually, I did not realize it had been in the My View column until two years later. I inadvertently came across it in reviewing other articles. I also am well aware that my modest proposal in the essay to cease eating animals on Earth Day is purely symbolic and has no effect on the world-wide suffering of our fellow creatures. I confess that I probably submitted the essay to stimulate thinking or perhaps even as an "irritant." A former parishioner of mine confirmed this when she read the essay and said it *was* irritating!

Forty years ago, a friend of mine encouraged me to read the book *Living the Good Life,* by Scott and Helen Nearing. This was my first serious encounter with the concept of vegetarianism. A few years later, I heard Scott speak at Amherst College and was again intrigued with his commitment to not eat or exploit animals. Twenty-eight years later, I found myself sitting in my car choking on a McDonald's barbecued rib sandwich and decided to move from being intrigued to taking action in regard to my eating habits. What follows is a comment on vegetarianism and my struggle in this matter.

The choking event in my car happened twenty years ago, and since that time I have wrestled with vegetarianism. My decision has been to cease eating my fellow mammals. When people ask me about my diet, and it does cause some stress and confusion in my relationships, I just say, "I don't eat animals."

There are three fundamental reasons why I have given up meat eating. The first is because of the suffering animals endure so we can eat them. In a small way, I don't want to be a part of this or support it. I read some years ago a statement by Linda McCartney. She and Paul were eating a Sunday dinner that included lamb chops and looked out the window to the lambs cavorting in the pasture near their country house. She said they looked at each other and suddenly realized what they were eating, and this became the beginning of their vegetarianism. Paul later said, "If slaughterhouses had glass walls, everyone would be a vegetarian." In this same vein Ralph Waldo Emerson wrote, "You have just dined, and however scrupulously the slaughterhouse is concealed in the graceful distance of miles, there is complicity." Having realized what suffering goes into meat eating, I am trying not to be any more complicit than I already am.

The second reason is because of health. Soon after giving up meat, I began to feel better. I had more energy, and my digestive functions were measurably improved. Einstein once wrote, "Nothing will benefit human health and increase chances of survival of life on Earth as much as the evolution to a vegetarian diet." And in her amazingly irritating way, Ingrid Newkirk of PETA said, "Recognize meat for what it really is: the antibiotic and pesticide-laden corpse of a tortured animal." I am convinced that not eating meat increases our health.

The third reason is one of solidarity with and a growing respect for animals. We have learned a good deal over the years of the ways animals show caring for each other and for humans. Albert Schweitzer tells the story of a flock of geese that settled to rest on a pond. When the flock was ready to resume their flight they realized that one had been injured. Even though the urge to go on was strong they waited for several days until the damaged goose found the strength to fly and then they resumed their long journey. Schweitzer said that this and other observations caused him to include animals in his Reverence for Life ethic. In writing about his early life he reports that when his mother left his bedroom following the Lord's Prayer he would add, "O Heavenly Father, protect and bless all things that have breath; guard them from all evil, and let them sleep in peace." What a wonderful addition to evening prayers!

There are also many stories of animals caring for humans. A few years ago we read of the little Down syndrome boy who was lost in the woods on a cold night. A stray dog stayed with him during the night and kept him warm, and when the ambulance took the child, the dog chased down the street after it. Many touching stories came as a result of the horror of the 9/11 attacks including that of Omar Eduardo Rivera, who was working on the seventy-first floor when the plane struck the building. Rivera is blind, and he unclipped his Seeing Eye dog, Salty, and sent him to freedom. A few moments passed, and Omar, resigned to his fate, felt a familiar nudge on his knee. Salty had come back, and he led his master down all those flights of stairs through the smoke to life. I find myself much more caring and respectful in regard to animals, and I enjoy them more now that I have stopped eating them.

We have much to learn about animals, and I believe that many years hence, the way we have treated animals in our age will be looked on as barbaric. Henry Beston in the *Outermost House* said that, "We need a wiser and perhaps more mystical concept of animals...they move finished and complete...living by voices we will never hear." I would also add that they are family and they deserve our moral and ethical consideration. After all, they are sentient beings in that they

117

have consciousness, a will to live, feelings, caring, and they do suffer.

Chapter eleven

WHAT SEEM SETBACKS, MAY BE GIFTS

July 22, 2011

This is the only body we have, and I strongly encourage all to celebrate and take care of this one time gift

WHAT SEEM SETBACKS
MAY BE GIFTS

JOHN RITTER OF *"Three's Company"*, Richard Holbrook our recent ambassador to Afghanistan, and Dick Williams former Red Sox manager of the 1967 World Series team all died when their aortic aneurysms ruptured. The ascending aorta is the large vessel that brings blood from the heart to the upper body and an aortic aneurysm is especially deadly because it is asymptomatic. As one surgeon said it is a silent ticking time bomb. These aneurysms are prone to rupture once they reach a certain size. 50% of patients who experience a rupture die before reaching the hospital. Surgical repair of a ruptured aortic aneurysm carries a

25-50% mortality risk as opposed to 5-8% when such aneurysms are treated electively.

Last November, during a routine echocardiogram it was discovered that I had an aneurysm on my ascending aorta. After seven months of further tests and much soul searching I elected to take an aggressive approach and have the aneurysm repaired. I didn't want the anxiety of wondering what might happen and I wanted to get back to an active lifestyle. The excellent surgical staff of the Cape Cod Hospital led by Dr. Robert Rizzo performed the operation and it was successful. I woke up from the anesthetic wondering if a truck had hit me but am now in the recovery stage. A week later, in my bed at night in the Spaulding Rehabilitation Hospital, I realized that I had been given two wonderful gifts---*gifts we all have but often ignore.*

The first gift was obvious. It was the return to me of some measure of control over my body. When we have a deadly illness we experience a loss of control and when we elect to enter into surgery we give ourselves over completely to others. I, as